# Whodunit?

## *How the Police Solve Crimes*

*by*
*Dori Hillestad Butler*

Perfection Learning®

Cover design: Deborah Lea Bell
Inside design and illustration: Dea Marks

**Dedication**
For my mom and dad

**About the Author**
Dori Hillestad Butler is a full-time writer and editor. She's sold 14 books for children as well as numerous magazine stories, educational pieces, book reviews, and Web stories. There's nothing she'd rather do than write.

Ms. Butler lives in Coralville, Iowa, with her husband and two sons. In her spare time she likes to walk, bike, read, and play Scrabble.

**Acknowledgement**

I would like to thank Doug Vance of the Coralville, Iowa, Police Department for showing me around the lab and taking the time to answer my numerous questions about police work.

The crime and the characters involved are strictly fictional.

Illustration: Dea Marks, pp. 17 (spatter) and 4, 10, 19, 28, 35, 40, 48 (chapter headings)

Image credits: ©Wally McNamee/CORBIS cover; ©MORELL JACQUES/CORBIS KIPA p. 23; ©Reuters NewMedia Inc./CORBIS p. 16; ©Hulton-Deutsch Collection/CORBIS p. 17 (bottom); AP/Wide World Photos pp. 15, 52

Clipart.com pp. 5, 7, 8, 9, 11, 17 (cotton swab), 19, 21 (bottom), 25, 29, 30 (background), 31 (background), 33, 34, 38, 47, 50; Corel Professional Photos p. 6 (top); Royalty-free/CORBIS pp. 31 (forefront), 43, 44, 46, 49, 51, 53, 54, 55; Photos.com pp. 18, 21 (top), 22, 30 (forefront), 32, 36, 37; Liquid Library pp. 6 (bottom), 12, 13, 24, 42–43; Photospin p. 41

Printed in the United States of America. For information, contact
Perfection Learning® Corporation, 1000 North Second Avenue,
P.O. Box 500, Logan, Iowa 51546-0500.
Tel: 1-800-831-4190 • Fax: 1-800-543-2745
perfectionlearning.com
Paperback ISBN 0-7891-6026-9
Cover Craft® ISBN 0-7569-1373-x

1 2 3 4 5 6 PP 08 07 06 05 04 03

# Table of Contents

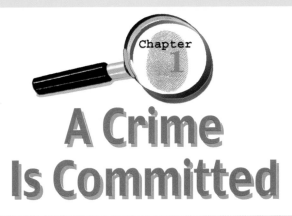

# A Crime Is Committed

Something was wrong with Tyler's bike. It rode as if the tires were rolling in wet cement. He just couldn't get up to speed.

"Hey! Wait up!" Tyler called to his sister.

Tyler wheeled over to the curb, got off his bike, and squeezed the front tire. It felt a little low. He squeezed the back tire. It felt a *lot* low.

Beth turned her bike around and rode back to him. "What's the matter, Tyler?" she asked.

"I think my tires need some air," Tyler answered.

Beth and Tyler looked around. "There's a Gas-N-Shop over there." Beth pointed at a convenience store up ahead.

"They probably have an air pump," Tyler said. He mounted his bike and followed Beth to the Gas-N-Shop.

They rode between the gas pumps and across the empty parking lot. A big white sign that read AIR was attached to the side of the building.

Tyler twisted the cap off his front tire. Beth pulled out the hose. But before they could attach the hose to his tire, they heard a strange popping sound. The sound came from inside the Gas-N-Shop. Beth and Tyler looked at each other.

"What was that?" Beth asked.

"I don't know," Tyler answered.

They walked around to the front of the building.

*Pop! Pop!*

The door to the Gas-N-Shop flew open. A man ran out. Even though it was the middle of summer, he was wearing a weird cloth over his face. The cloth made him look as if he didn't have any eyes or mouth—just a hump where his nose was.

He had a gun in his hand. He pointed it right at Beth and Tyler. The man looked at them.

Suddenly, a red car zoomed into the parking lot. The driver honked the horn, and the man with the gun turned. He ran to the car and jumped in. The car sped away.

"D—did that man just rob the Gas-N-Shop?" Beth asked. She inched closer to the door.

"I don't know. But we shouldn't go in," Tyler said. "We don't know who else might be in there with a gun."

Tyler reached into his side pocket and pulled out his mom's cell phone. He was sure glad he had it. Mom always made them take it when they went for bike rides.

Tyler flipped the phone open and pushed 911.

# 911—What Is It?

The national emergency telephone number is 911. Whether people live in Los Angeles, Minneapolis, or Boston, they can dial 911 for any emergency.

When a person dials 911, the call goes to a local answering center. The center is located in a police station or another communication center. The person who answers the call is called a *dispatcher*. This person's job is to find out what the emergency is and to send help.

# Enhanced 911 Systems

Some communities use an "enhanced" 911 system. Enhanced 911 systems allow dispatchers to see the addresses and phone numbers of callers. This is especially helpful when the callers are children or if they speak languages that the dispatchers don't. It is also helpful if the callers are in dangerous situations.

If calls are made from cell phones, addresses won't register on the system. Dispatchers then rely on the callers to give that information.

# Why 911?

No one knows for sure why 911 was chosen for the national emergency number. There were probably several reasons.

- It was an easy sequence to dial on a rotary telephone.
- When the system was invented, there were no area codes in the United States that began with 9.
- Perhaps it also had something to do with the fact that Great Britain's national emergency number is 999.

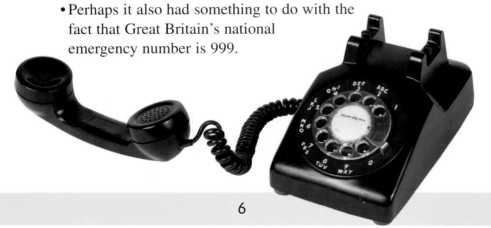

# Before 911

Before the 911 system was available, people needing emergency services had to look up a seven-digit number in a phone book. If they needed to report a robbery, they'd call the police department. If they needed to report a fire, they'd call the fire department.

The problem with seven-digit emergency numbers was that it took time to find the correct number. In some large cities, more than 200 numbers were listed for various public-safety agencies. It was hard to know which was the right number to call.

Most telephone companies offered a dial-operator service. People could dial 0, and operators would connect the callers with the local police, fire, or ambulance department. But it often took time for the operators to find the correct numbers.

In an emergency, every second counts. The 911 system allows people to get the help they need fast.

## The First 911 Call

B. W. Gallagher, president of the Alabama Telephone Company, installed the first 911 system in the United States in Haleyville, Alabama. The first 911 call was made at 2:00 p.m. on Friday, February 16, 1968. Alabama Speaker of the House Rankin Fite placed the call from the mayor's office in Haleyville. U.S. Representative Tom Bevill answered it at the Haleyville police station. Fite and Bevill greeted each other and then hung up. The red telephone that Bevill used to take the call is on display at the Haleyville police station.

## Does 911 Work Everywhere?

Every major city in the United States and Canada has access to 911. This number can even be dialed from a pay phone without depositing money.

But the 911 service is not available everywhere. As of 2002, some remote areas in more than 20 states did not have the system. If a person dials 911 in an area where the service is not available, a recording tells the caller to look up the emergency number in a phone book.

## When a Crime Has Been Committed

When a person dials 911, a dispatcher logs, or records, the time the call comes in and asks what type of emergency is being reported. For example, if the emergency is a robbery, the dispatcher asks the exact location.

The dispatcher also wants to make sure the caller is safe. Depending on the situation, the caller may be asked to leave the area. If that is not possible, the caller is told to stay out of sight, preferably in a locked room.

With calls such as Tyler's, the dispatcher asks many questions until the police arrive. Is the suspect still there? Is the suspect armed? Is anyone else inside the store? Has anyone been hurt? Are there any suspicious people or vehicles around? Did anyone leave the scene?

The dispatcher asks about the suspect—age, sex, race, height, weight, hair color, hairstyle, and clothing. The caller is also asked whether the person left on foot or in a vehicle. If a vehicle was used, the caller is asked to describe it.

While the caller answers the questions, the dispatcher contacts the police and sends them to the scene. The dispatcher also relays all the information from the caller to police officers.

When the police arrive, they take over the situation. The dispatcher then has the caller hang up.

# Chapter 2

# The Crime Scene

Police officers arrived quickly. Some of them wore uniforms. Others didn't. They talked on their radios and watched the door to the Gas-N-Shop.

"We need to secure the area," ordered the officer in charge. "Keep the bystanders back. And I need to get a description of this guy from the witnesses."

"Are you the one who called 911?" the officer asked Tyler.

"Yes," he said.

"I'm Detective Walker. What's your name?"

"Tyler," the boy answered. "This is my sister—Beth." They shook hands with Detective Walker.

Detective Walker continued asking questions. "Did you see anybody come out of the Gas-N-Shop?"

"Yes," Tyler replied. "A man ran out."

"Did you see where he went? Which direction?" the detective asked.

Beth and Tyler pointed. "That way."

The detective smiled and asked, "Was he in a vehicle or on foot?"

"In a vehicle," Beth and Tyler said together.

"He got in a red car and took off," Tyler added.

Right away, four patrol officers ran to their cars. They zoomed away while several other officers entered the store.

"Do you know whether anyone is inside the Gas-N-Shop?" Detective Walker continued.

"I don't know," Tyler said.

By now, quite a few people had gathered near the Gas-N-Shop parking lot. Some were just regular people who had stopped to see what was going on.

"We need an ambulance," an officer called from the door of the Gas-N-Shop. "It looks like the cashier has been shot."

"I'll call it in." Detective Walker reached for her cell phone.

## Teamwork

A lot of teamwork is used at a crime scene. The highest-ranking officer on the scene is in charge and decides who is going to do what.

Patrol officers secure the crime scene. They stretch yellow tape around the area to keep out curious bystanders as well as the media. It's important that all the evidence remain untouched. Just walking through a crime scene can destroy evidence.

Patrol officers also write down the names, addresses, dates of birth, and phone numbers of everyone who happens to be in the area. They also record the license numbers of every vehicle parked on the street and in parking lots nearby.

Other patrol officers drive around looking for the person who committed the crime. They check dumpsters in the area in case the suspect threw away clothes, weapons, or other evidence.

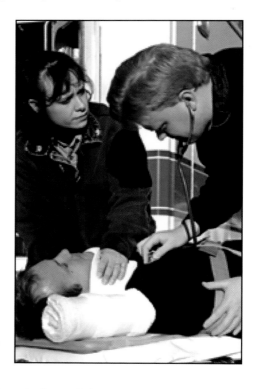

In this case, an ambulance arrives for the cashier who has been shot. An officer rides along to the hospital. If possible, the officer will ask the victim for information.

Police officers and detectives use cell phones and radios to keep in touch with one another and with the dispatcher. If the cashier gives the officer a description of the suspect, the officer passes it on to the police patrolling the streets. If the cashier tells the officer the suspect picked up a can of Coke, the officer tells the detectives at the Gas-N-Shop to look for it. The can is then fingerprinted.

The officer also gathers evidence at the hospital. This includes a copy of the cashier's medical records, photographs, clothing, and X-rays. The X-ray might show a bullet inside his body. The charges that will be filed against the suspect will depend on how badly the cashier is injured.

Back at the Gas-N-Shop, the investigators watch videotapes from the store's security cameras. They hope the suspect appears on the tapes. Other patrol officers are alerted to any additional information about the suspect's description.

The videotape might show the criminal handling merchandise inside the convenience store. The detectives will find and fingerprint those items.

Solving a crime requires teamwork. Many people must work together to solve a crime and see that justice is served.

## Don't Touch Anything

The police want to know if any items at the crime scene have been moved. If so, what were they, who moved them, and why?

Officers keep their hands at their sides and step carefully when they walk into a crime scene. They may even wear shoe covers to make sure they don't destroy any evidence. They don't use the phone, flush the toilet, run water, or smoke. They don't allow anyone to come in or go out until all the evidence has been gathered.

The investigators write down whether the lights are on or off, whether doors are open or closed, and whether the doors are locked or unlocked. They also note where the cashier was lying. They record the date, time, and current weather. It may be important later to know whether it was sunny, cloudy, or windy and whether it had rained recently.

# Locard's Exchange Principle

Edmond Locard was a French scientist who lived from 1877 to 1966. His laboratory was the first modern crime lab in the world. He is sometimes called the "father of criminalistics." Criminalistics is the use of scientific techniques to collect and study physical evidence found at a crime scene.

Locard believed that whenever two objects came together, there was always some part of each object that was picked up by the other object. This is known as "Locard's Exchange Principle."

When a person walks into a room, tiny bits of that person are left behind—hair, skin cells, and clothing fibers. And when the person leaves, tiny bits from the room are picked up—carpet fibers, hairs, and so on. These are all examples of trace evidence. Trace evidence can be studied and can possibly lead to an arrest.

## Photographing the Scene

Before police gather any evidence, the entire area is photographed. Usually the detective who photographs the scene is the same person who collects the evidence. It's better if just one person gathers all the evidence. If several people are assigned to the task, it's more likely something might be missed.

The detective starts by photographing outside. Pictures are taken of the crime scene from a distance. These pictures show where the crime took place and the surrounding area.

The people who are standing around are also photographed. Sometimes a suspect shows up in photographs of a crowd milling around the crime scene.

When the photographer enters a crime scene, distant shots are taken first. Then the photographer zooms in for closer ones.

Each piece of evidence is photographed before it is

gathered. Pictures are also taken of fingerprints before they're lifted. Pictures are taken of every drop of blood, any shell casings, footprints, extra clothing, or any other items that are found at the crime scene.

A numbered square is placed beside each piece of evidence. Someone else writes down the number and the item. The scene is photographed with the numbers and without the numbers. The photos show where and how the evidence was found.

Once the detective is sure the entire scene has been photographed, the evidence is gathered.

## Gathering Evidence

A detective isn't always sure whether an item is going to be important to solving the crime. More evidence than is actually used in a case is usually collected. A detective must treat everything as if it were important.

In a convenience store robbery, the detective fingerprints the door. People often don't use the door handle when they leave. They just put their hands right on the glass and push the door open.

The detective also looks for shoe prints, both in and around the scene. People usually have to run a short distance to leave the area. Along the way, the suspect may have run through a mud puddle or over some gravel. Shoe prints in mud or gravel can be plastered.

**Plaster**
Plaster is a mixture of lime or gypsum, sand, and water that hardens into a smooth surface.

Detectives often pour plaster over shoe prints or tire tracks that are found at a crime scene. When the plaster hardens, it leaves a cast of the print.

If shoe prints are found at the scene, they might show mud, dirt, or oil brought from outside. Or they might contain blood. A detective photographs any shoe prints after placing a flat measuring stick beside each print to show how big it is.

Any tire tracks found outside are plastered, and any skid marks are photographed.

If drops of blood are found, three samples are taken from each location. Where blood is found is more important than the amount of blood. A detective makes sure samples are collected from each location. A large cotton swab is used to lift the blood. The swab is then placed inside a paper bag or envelope.

### Blood Spatter

Blood spatter tells what happened. The shape of each drop of blood is measured and photographed. The shape and spacing of drops of blood can tell detectives how fast the victim was moving, how many blows the victim received, how close the victim was to another object when blood was shed, and where the victim was when blood was first shed.

Any item or surface that the suspect may have touched is dusted for fingerprints. Some evidence is taken from the scene, such as notes, shell casings from a gun, money, gloves, or other items that seem important.

### Dusting

Detectives sprinkle a fine powder over a surface that contains a fingerprint. The powder will stick to the print. Then the detectives brush the excess powder away and use a wide tape to lift the print.

In the case of convenience store robberies, suspects don't just walk inside the store and rob it. They usually pick something up—a soft drink can, a candy bar, or a magazine—and then they approach the cashier.

Each piece of evidence is labeled and put into a bag. Most evidence is collected in paper bags. Too much moisture can collect inside plastic bags, which damages the evidence. The detective will also note exactly where an item was found and how it was lying when it was found.

When detectives gather evidence, they follow certain rules. All evidence must be bagged and labeled in a certain way. If it is passed to another person, both parties must sign a slip. This is known as the chain of evidence. Police must have control of all evidence from the time it is collected until it is needed in court. If these rules are not followed, the evidence cannot be used.

## Using the Scientific Method

Detectives are scientists. They use a scientific method to find out what happened, when it happened, where it happened, how it happened, why it happened, and who did it.

They follow certain steps in order to answer these questions. First, they gather as much information as they can. Then they study all the information they have. They look for errors or things that don't make sense. They ask lots of questions.

Next, detectives form a hypothesis, or what they think happened. They test their hypothesis in all possible ways. When they think they have enough evidence, they arrest the suspect.

# Interviewing Witnesses

"Okay, Tyler," Detective Walker said. She pulled out a small notepad and started writing. "Let's start at the beginning. You noticed your bike tires were a little low. So you and your sister decided to stop here at the Gas-N-Shop."

"That's right," Tyler said.

"What did you see when you first arrived?" the detective asked.

Tyler looked at Beth. She was talking with another officer by the air pump. Tyler was on his own. "We didn't really see anything at first," he answered.

"Nobody was pumping gas?" the detective questioned.

"No, ma'am," he responded.

Then she asked, "Were there any cars in the parking lot at all?"

Tyler shook his head. "I don't think so. But I really can't remember for sure."

"So you rode over to the air pump." Detective Walker pointed. "What happened then?"

Tyler thought for a moment. "Well, I was about to put air in my front tire when I heard this loud popping noise."

"How many popping noises did you hear?" The detective's gaze was fixed on the boy.

"I don't know," Tyler answered. "Three? Maybe four?" How many had Beth heard? he wondered.

Detective Walker was writing all this down. Tyler didn't want to tell her anything wrong.

"And then what?" she asked.

"A man ran out of the store," he replied.

"What did he look like? Close your eyes and think about the man," she said.

"He was tall and really thin," Tyler said. "I think he had brown hair. I couldn't really see his face, though. He had some sort of a cloth over it."

"What kind of cloth?" the detective prodded.

"I don't know." Then Tyler added, "Not a winter ski mask kind of thing. It was thinner than that."

"What color was it?" she asked Tyler.

Tyler had to think about that. "It looked like skin."

Just then another police officer came over to them. He had a beige cloth in his hand. "We found this in the street over there," he told Detective Walker. Then he turned to Tyler. "Do you recognize this?"

Tyler gasped. "That's it!" he said. "That's what the guy was wearing over his face!"

## Interviewing on the Scene

A witness is anybody who may have seen or heard something. Anybody who was in the area when a crime took place may be a witness.

Officers talk with every possible person, even those who claim they didn't see anything. People often think they didn't see anything, but they still may be able to give important information. If they live or work in the area, perhaps they know something about the area that other people don't. Or perhaps they noticed strange people or vehicles in the area. It's impossible to know which pieces of information will turn out to be important later on.

Many people don't want to get involved. It doesn't matter whether they saw something or not. Some people don't "have time." They don't want to wait around to be questioned. And they don't want to go to court.

Other people simply prefer to keep to themselves. What happened to somebody else doesn't concern them.

Still others are afraid to become involved. They worry that the person who committed the crime will come after them if they talk to the police.

Some people are simply nervous about talking to the police in general. Some don't like police officers. Or they may have committed a similar crime in the past. They may be innocent of the current crime, but they fear they might become suspects.

But other people want to be involved. They don't know anything about the crime. But they pretend that they know more than they do. They may even make things up just to have a chance to talk to the police. This makes them feel like part of the action.

Some people, such as Tyler and Beth, are willing to tell police what they witnessed. They don't want crimes to go unsolved and criminals to remain free.

Police officers must listen to what *all* witnesses tell them. Then they must judge how reliable the information is.

## What Kinds of Questions Do the Police Ask?

Police officers often begin by simply making conversation. They might talk about the weather or about local sports teams. They might ask whether the witness is married or has kids. They want the person to feel comfortable.

Then the interviewers ask the important questions. Why were you in the area? What did you see? Were there cars in the parking lot? Were there any people around? Where were you standing? What happened? What happened next? The goal is to get as many details as possible.

**Interviewing**

Interviewers want witnesses to do most of the talking. Most of the questions they ask are open-ended questions that can't be answered with a simple yes or no.

The interviewer pays close attention to not only what the witness says, but how the person acts. Is the witness making eye contact with the interviewer? Or is the person looking off to the side? Does the witness appear tense or relaxed? Are the person's arms crossed or down at the sides? Is the witness sitting still or moving around? These are all clues to how reliable the witness is.

## Later Interviews

As detectives gather more information, they may find they need to talk to witnesses a second time. Or one witness may lead them to new witnesses.

Detectives prefer that these later interviews take place at the police station rather than at the witnesses' homes or jobs. Most people are willing to come to the station to talk.

Some witnesses become suspects. A suspect is someone the police think committed a crime, but they don't have enough evidence to prove it. The detectives hope that by bringing the person down to the station they can learn more information. The investigator goes over the suspect's story—piece by piece. A lot of questions are asked.

If not officially in police custody, the suspect can get up and walk out at any time. The person can simply say, "I don't feel like talking anymore." Unless the suspect is placed under arrest, the police must let that person go.

But sometimes the police get lucky, and the suspect confesses.

## When Suspects Lie

Very few guilty people come right out and admit they committed a crime. Detectives have to look for clues that a suspect isn't telling the whole truth.

If something doesn't sound right or feel right, the detective may ask the person to start at the end and work backward. It's easy to lie when thinking forward in time. But when asked to begin at the end and move to the beginning, the person has more difficulty telling a lie.

Detectives also understand that people who are telling the truth will usually give appropriate answers to questions. People who are lying may give inappropriate answers. For instance, a detective might say, "If you wanted to rob a convenience store, how would you go about it?" An honest person may appear uncomfortable by the question. But that person would likely go on to say how a person might commit the crime. A person who really did commit the crime would probably reply, "I would never do that." The response is inappropriate. It doesn't answer the question.

A detective might ask, "If we catch this guy who robbed the Gas-N-Shop, what do you think should happen to him?" Someone who is not guilty would probably say, "The person should go to jail." But someone who is guilty might say, "No one got killed. If the person is really sorry, probation would be enough. Give the person another chance."

At this point, the detective may think the suspect is guilty. But if there isn't enough proof, an arrest can't be made. The only hope is to get the suspect to admit to the crime.

Detectives try several things. They might get right in the suspect's face and say, "I know you did it! Why don't you just admit it?"

Or they might use a gentler approach by saying, "Listen, I know you just lost your job. You don't have any money. You have a wife and three kids to feed. You're not a bad person. You didn't mean for anyone to get hurt. You just wanted to feed your family. Isn't that why you robbed the Gas-N-Shop today?"

Sometimes these methods cause a suspect to confess. Sometimes they don't. Often the suspect just stands up and leaves.

## Interview vs. Interrogation

An interview and an interrogation are similar. Both involve a conversation with a witness or suspect. The goal is to get information. But an interview is more relaxed than an interrogation.

One detective said, "An interview is when I ask questions and the suspect answers them. But an interrogation is where I do all the talking. The only thing I want to hear out of the suspect is 'I did it.' "

Interrogation is a style of communication. It involves control. When detectives interrogate witnesses or suspects, they are pretty sure that the person is guilty of the crime. The goal of an interrogation is a confession.

Sometimes an interview turns into an interrogation. The detective will read the suspect his rights. At this point the suspect is not free to leave.

# Miranda Rights

The Miranda warning reads

*You have the right to remain silent.*

*Anything you say can and will be used against you in a court of law.*

*You have the right to speak to an attorney, and to have an attorney present during any questioning.*

*If you cannot afford an attorney, one will be provided for you.*

Detectives must inform a suspect of these rights before an interrogation. If they don't, whatever the person says cannot be used in court.

The police don't have to read Miranda rights the moment they arrest someone. But they have to do it if they ask questions and intend to use the information they gain in court.

Miranda rights are not read to witnesses who come in for an interview. These people are not in police custody and are free to leave at any time.

## Getting Statements

Taking statements means recording what witnesses say so the information can be used in court. At this time, detectives often ask the witnesses questions that require a simple yes or no. Sometimes the witnesses are asked to tell in their own words what they know about a crime.

Once detectives finish recording statements, the witnesses are asked whether they were threatened, whether any promises were made, and whether they were forced to make their statements. Then the statements are typed, and the witnesses sign them.

**Notarized Statements**

The statements that witnesses sign are notarized. This means that the statement was signed in the presence of a person who is legally authorized to guarantee that all necessary procedures have been followed correctly. These statements can be used in court.

Sworn to and subscribed before me this _____ day of _____, _____ by: John Doe
NOTARY PUBLIC

# Chapter 4

# The Lab

"So, what do we have?" Detective Walker asked. She and the other detectives and officers gathered in a conference room at police headquarters to talk about the case.

"We have a couple of partial shoe prints," Detective Roberts said. "Two outside. One inside. Also some fingerprints. Some from the front door, the counter, and a refrigerator door handle. Some are from a can of Coke left on the counter."

"Was our guy wearing gloves at the time?" Detective Kerr asked.

"Don't know," Detective Roberts replied. "Can't tell from the store videotape. And the cashier doesn't remember."

"Neither do the kids," Detective Walker added.

"We also have a couple of shell casings and a bullet that was recovered from the cashier's shoulder," said Officer Peters.

"How's he doing?" asked Detective Walker.

"Pretty well," the officer replied. "He was lucky. Only one bullet struck him. And it was lodged in his shoulder. He's going to need some therapy, but he'll be okay."

"What do we know about the gun?" asked Officer Kerr.

"It's a 9-mm handgun," Detective Roberts answered.

"What else do we have?" asked Detective Walker.

"We found a painter's mask in the garbage can by the first gas pump," Officer Warren said. "Those kids were pretty sure our guy was wearing one just like it."

"We found a pair of latex gloves in there too," Officer Morgan added.

"Send the mask and gloves in to the state crime lab," Detective Walker told the officers. "See if we can get some DNA."

"We're still talking to people too," Detective Roberts offered.

"Any leads yet?" Detective Walker asked.

"Not yet," replied Detective Roberts. "But we'll keep working."

## Fingerprints

If you look at the tips of your own fingers you'll see lots of ridges. Those ridges form patterns of arches, loops, and whorls. No two people have exactly the same ridge detail. In fact, if you ever lose part of the skin on the tip of your finger, the ridges will grow back in the same pattern as before.

Dactyloscopy is the scientific study of fingerprints. Fingerprints are often used to identify criminals.

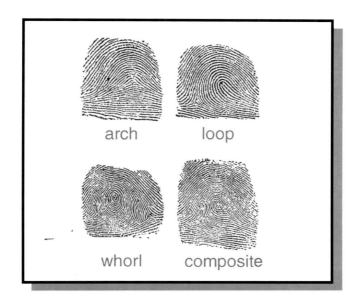

arch    loop

whorl    composite

# Kinds of Fingerprints

Criminals may leave behind several different kinds of fingerprints at a crime scene.

1. Plastic prints are prints that leave an indentation in something else. The print may be stuck in wet paint, gum, butter, grease, or some other substance.

2. Patent prints are those that are made when dirty fingers touch a clean surface. For example, a finger with blood on it will leave a bloody print. A finger with ink on it will leave an ink print.

3. Latent prints are prints that you cannot see. They're made with the sweat and natural oils found in your skin. They're found on smooth surfaces or on paper.

## Lifting Fingerprints

More than 40 ways exist to lift fingerprints. One of the most common ways is dusting with fingerprint powder. The powder

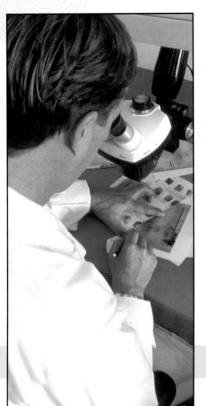

may be any color. If the object that contains the fingerprint is dark, detectives use a light powder. If the object is light, detectives use a dark powder. Some detectives like to use a fluorescent powder because it makes a nice picture when they go to court.

Detectives use feather brushes with long, fine bristles to dust for fingerprints. They dust the powder over the prints. Before they lift the prints, they photograph them. Then they use wide tape to lift the prints from the surface. The tape is stuck to a card or between plastic sheets.

If the prints are on something metal, detectives use metal filings to get the print. Metal filings also show up well on plastic and on shiny objects like magazine covers.

Detectives also use superglue to get fingerprints. The object with a print is placed in a covered container with a heat source. (This source can be a 60-watt lightbulb.) A small amount of superglue is placed in the container also. When heated, the superglue becomes a vapor or fog. This fog sticks to the object and makes the print visible. Using superglue seals the print so it can be lifted from the object more than once.

Different chemicals are used to make fingerprints show up on wood or paper. Ninhydrin is one. This chemical soaks into the object, so it can't be used on metal. But it does lift fingerprints from checks or other papers.

Some liquids can be used on wet surfaces. Powders aren't used because they just make a mess. But solutions, such as small particle reagent, are mixed and sprayed on a wet surface. The surface is then rinsed with clear water. The water washes away everything except the print.

## Making a Match

A fingerprint by itself isn't very useful. Somebody needs to match it to a suspect. How do detectives do that?

They start by comparing fingerprints they found at the crime scene to fingerprints they already have on file. Anybody who has ever been arrested has been fingerprinted.

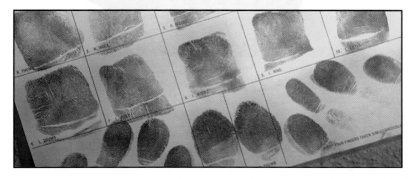

But when a person is fingerprinted after being arrested, only the fingertips are printed. Fingerprints that are lifted at a crime scene may be from the side of the finger. In order to match those prints, detectives need a suspect from whom they can take samples.

When detectives compare fingerprints, they're looking for unique points that appear on both prints. They need at least seven identical points before fingerprints are considered a match. They prefer ten to twelve points.

## Identifying Shoe Prints

In addition to fingerprints, detectives sometimes find shoe prints at a crime scene. Shoe prints are actually more common than fingerprints. Criminals often wear gloves to avoid leaving fingerprints. But very few will put something over their shoes.

Shoe prints may be found outside in dirt, mud, or snow. Or they may be found inside if the criminal has tracked in dirt.

Detectives look at shoe print photographs and plaster molds to identify the shoe. They'll look at shoe brands, types, styles, and designs. Next, they'll look at the cuts and scratches on the individual print. Perhaps a small pebble is stuck in the tread. Or maybe the print shows a certain pattern of wear. These characteristics help detectives link shoe prints to suspects.

Just because detectives prove a person's shoe was at a crime scene doesn't make that person guilty. All it proves is that the suspect's shoe was there. But the suspect needs to explain why the shoe print was found at the scene.

## Tire Tracks

Detectives also look at tire tracks or skid marks that may have been left at a crime scene. They measure how wide the tracks are and the distance between them. This tells them how large the vehicle is.

Just like fingerprints and shoe prints, tire tracks are different. When a vehicle drives over a sharp object, the object may leave a mark on the tire. Pebbles and other debris stick in the tire treads. Everything that happens to a tire leaves a mark.

Again, tire tracks don't prove that a person committed a crime. But they can prove that a person, or at least that person's vehicle, was at the crime scene.

## Guns

The inside of a gun barrel is also similar to a fingerprint or shoe print. There are ridges and grooves that form a spiral path on the bullet as it travels through the gun barrel. These ridges and grooves are all different. As a bullet passes through the barrel, a series of spiral marks is cut into it. Detectives can match the marks on a bullet to the gun from which it was fired. No two gun barrels are exactly alike.

When a suspect's gun is found, it is sent to a crime lab along with any bullets from the crime scene. An examiner fires the gun several  times into a box filled with cotton or into a tank of water. Then the marks on these bullets are compared with the marks on the bullet found at the crime scene.

Unfortunately, it isn't always easy to find bullets at a crime scene. And even if bullets are found, they're often damaged. They may be smashed or broken apart. It may not be possible to match these bullets to a gun.

However, as a bullet travels through an object, it picks up small particles from that object. For example, pieces of dirt, wood, clothing, or bone may be stuck inside the smashed head of a bullet. These pieces tell where the bullet has been.

## Photo Enhancement

Sometimes a crime, such as a convenience store robbery, is caught on videotape. This tape can solve a crime by showing exactly what happened and who was involved.

But sometimes the quality of the tape isn't very good. The image may be blurry and detectives can't see the criminal clearly.

When that happens, the image can often be digitally enhanced. That means it's run through a computer. The computer makes a blurry image sharp. It can also zoom in on a small part of the picture and make it bigger. Sometimes it can zoom in close enough to show a scar on the suspect's face or some other unique feature that may help detectives identify the suspect.

# Digging Deeper

"Any word yet from the crime lab?" Detective Walker asked.

"Not yet," Detective Roberts replied.

Detective Walker frowned. "Let me know when it comes in."

"Do you have something?" Detective Roberts asked her.

"Maybe," Detective Walker answered. "I've been talking to a detective in Springfield. Seems someone robbed the Gas-N-Shop there. They have DNA that ties their guy to the person who robbed another store in Bloomington. The guy was caught there, but the jury didn't convict. He walked. But we have a name."

Detective Roberts smiled at the news. "What is it?"

"Reese. Derek Reese," replied Detective Walker.

Detective Roberts shook his head. "Don't know him."

"Neither do I," said Detective Walker. "But there's a Derek Reese living in a house on First Avenue. We've never picked him up here, but he has a couple of assault charges on his record. And he owns a red Ford Taurus."

"A red Ford Taurus?" Detective Roberts sat up a little straighter. "We had those kids come in and look at pictures of cars. They think the suspect probably drove away in a red Taurus."

"They sure did," Detective Walker replied. "If there's any DNA in the gloves or on the mask and that DNA matches what they have in Springfield and Bloomington, we might want to pay a little visit to Mr. Reese."

"Like a 'welcome to our community' visit?" Detective Roberts asked with a smirk.

"Something like that," Detective Walker laughed.

# DNA

DNA evidence is being used more and more to solve crimes. It is possible to get DNA samples from skin tissue, blood, urine, sweat, saliva, bones, hair, and teeth. In the convenience store case, detectives cut away the part of the painter's mask that covered the criminal's mouth and sent that in to the state crime lab. They hope traces of saliva will be found on that cloth. If so, DNA can be taken. There may also be DNA inside the gloves. The gloves were latex, so there may be sweat inside.

**What Is DNA?**

DNA stands for deoxyribonucleic acid. DNA is a molecule found in all living cells. Each cell contains an organism's entire genetic code. DNA is what makes you who you are. It gives you two eyes, two ears, a heart, and so on. It determines whether you are tall or short and whether you have brown eyes or blue eyes. DNA makes you unique.

DNA result sample

A DNA sample looks like a grocery store bar code. It is made up of patterns of light and dark bands. There are more than ten million spots on a DNA strand that can be different. It's highly unlikely that two people have the same DNA. Only the DNA of identical twins would be the same.

Investigators compare DNA samples found at a crime scene with samples from a suspect and prove whether the person was there or not.

## Guilty or Innocent?

DNA evidence was used against a suspect in the 1993 World Trade Center bombing. *The New York Times* received a letter from the "Liberation Army" claiming responsibility for the attack. The letter was typed on a personal computer and printed on a laser printer. DNA evidence on the envelope proved that a man named Nidel Ayyad, who was already a suspect in the case, had licked the envelope.

DNA evidence has also been used to prove that a suspect is innocent. For instance, in 1984, Kirk Bloodsworth was accused of murdering a 9-year-old girl. He had no criminal record. He claimed he was innocent. But a jury disagreed. They felt the evidence proved he did it. He was sent to jail. Nine years later, DNA evidence proved he was indeed innocent.

In recent years, at least ten people have been freed from death row in the United States after DNA evidence later proved them innocent.

## Advantages and Disadvantages of DNA Testing

Some advantages of DNA testing include

DNA strand

1. It's accurate. Aside from identical twins, the odds of finding two people with the same DNA profile are somewhere between 100 million and 30 billion to one, depending on the number of strands of DNA tested.
2. DNA lasts for thousands of years. It can even be found on skeletal remains.
3. Any biological material can be tested. Detectives are not limited to blood samples.
4. It can prove a person innocent as well as guilty.
5. It may prove even more useful in the future. Eventually, DNA left at a crime scene may be able to tell detectives the person's race, eye and hair color, build, and so on.

Some disadvantages of DNA testing include

1. It's more expensive than regular blood testing.
2. It takes time. Most DNA testing is done in a separate lab, so it can take a while to receive results.
3. Different states have different laws about the use of DNA test results in court.
4. Explanations are complex. Juries may hear very different testimony about DNA from two different experts. This can be confusing.
5. There are no national standards.

## Other Sources of Information

Sometimes the police have evidence from a crime scene, but they have nobody to tie it to. Eyewitness reports didn't lead to a suspect. Or maybe the police had a suspect, but the evidence didn't match. What do they do then?

The officers check wanted posters. Maybe some of the people listed are wanted for crimes that are similar. They look at similar crimes that have been committed. Or they read through journals of unsolved crimes. If they see a crime that sounds similar to the crime they're trying to solve, they contact the police department where that crime was committed. If the two departments talk and compare evidence, they may find something in common.

Sometimes finding the criminal is just luck. The police may arrest someone on a completely different matter. Then that person will offer information on another crime if the police agree to go easy on charges for this arrest.

No matter what the information is or where it comes from, the police check it all.

# Chapter 6

# Putting It All Together

Derek Reese lived in a small brick house. Some of the bricks were crumbling. The screen on the front door was torn.

"Looks like these people need to do some home repair," said Detective Roberts. Detective Walker knocked on the door. The detectives made sure their badges were visible.

The man who came to the door looked similar to the man caught on the videotape at the Gas-N-Shop. And he matched the description Beth and Tyler had given. He was tall and thin. He had dark hair.

"Yeah?" the man said. He didn't look happy to see police officers on his doorstep.

"Are you Derek Reese?" Detective Walker asked.

"Yeah. What do you want?" the man growled.

"May we come in and talk to you?" Detective Walker asked.

Instead of inviting the detectives inside, Reese stepped outside. He pulled his front door closed behind him. "So, what do you want?" he asked again.

"Are you familiar with the Gas-N-Shop over on Broadway?" Detective Walker asked.

"What about it?" answered Reese.

"It was robbed last week," Detective Roberts said. He watched Reese's face closely.

Reese folded his arms across his chest. "I don't know anything about that."

"I don't suppose you know anything about a robbery at the Gas-N-Shop in Springfield a few months ago, either?" Detective Roberts asked.

"Nope," the man answered.

"Where were you the morning of July 20 around 10:00 a.m.?" Detective Walker asked.

Reese shrugged. "I don't know. Probably at home."

"Was anybody here with you at the time?" Detective Roberts asked.

"Nope. I live alone," Reese said.

"Do you mind if we come in and have a look around?" Detective Walker asked.

"You got a warrant?" Reese sneered.

## Search Warrants

The Fourth Amendment of the U.S. Constitution says

*The right of the people to be secure in their persons, houses, papers, and effects, against unreasonable searches and seizures, shall not be violated, and no warrants shall issue, but upon probable cause, supported by oath or affirmation, and particularly describing the place to be searched, and the person or things to be seized.*

That means the police can't search a suspect's home or car or any other property without first getting a warrant.

To get a warrant, police officers or detectives must show probable cause. In other words, they must be pretty sure a crime has been committed and the suspect is involved. They state what they are looking for and why they think it is at this particular location. The detectives can only take items that they have specifically asked for in the warrant.

Detectives need a judge to issue a warrant. But that depends on the laws of their city. In most cases, it can take anywhere from one to three hours to get a warrant.

## Means, Motive, and Opportunity

Detectives may think they know who committed a crime. But they cannot arrest the suspect just because they think that person did it. They need proof. They need to prove that this person had the means, motive, and opportunity to commit the crime.

- **Means:** Could this person have committed this crime? Did the suspect have the right tools? Did the suspect have the knowledge? If a gun was involved, did the suspect have a gun? Did this person know how to use it?

- **Motive:** Would this person have a reason for committing this crime? In the convenience store case, is the suspect out of work and needing money? Or does the suspect have a problem with the store owner?

- **Opportunity:** Could this person have been at the scene when the crime was committed? If the suspect claims to have been somewhere else, is there anybody who can verify the alibi, or excuse?

# Making an Arrest

In most cases, police need an arrest warrant before they can arrest a suspect. Like a search warrant, an arrest warrant comes from a judge. It must name the person being arrested. It also must name the crime for which the person is being arrested.

Detectives must show probable cause in order to get the warrant. They must list details that prove the suspect likely committed the crime. For instance, evidence such as a weapon was found at the suspect's home. The suspect matches the description of witnesses or was identified in a lineup or from a photograph. The suspect has no alibi—someone to say the suspect was somewhere else.

An arrest warrant is not needed if the person has committed a crime in front of an officer. Also, if the police think the suspect might escape, destroy evidence, or kill someone, then a warrant is not needed.

Once an arrest warrant has been issued, any officer can make the arrest. The arrest warrant doesn't expire. The person can be arrested anytime—even years later.

When a person is about to be arrested at home, the officers knock on the door. They must identify themselves and name who is about to be arrested. If the person refuses to open the door, the officers can break a door or window to enter.

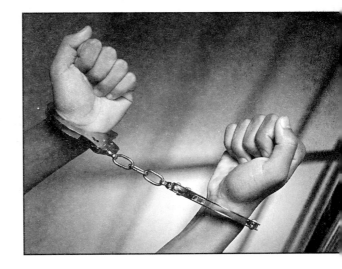

**No-Knock Warrant**

Officers can have a judge issue a no-knock warrant if they can show a judge they need one for personal safety. This means that the officers can enter a home without identifying themselves.

Resisting arrest is also a crime. If the person refuses to go with the officer, charges of resisting arrest can be added.

When a person is arrested, police may search the area within reach of the person. In other words, if that person is arrested in a car, police may search the car. If the person is arrested outdoors, police may not search the person's house or car without a search warrant.

## What Happens Next?

What happens when somebody is arrested depends on the crime. Generally, the suspect—now the accused—is taken to the police station and booked. That means the accused is searched, photographed, and fingerprinted. Somebody also logs the accused person's name and the time of arrival at the station.

The accused is usually allowed to make a phone call to a lawyer or to arrange bail.

Detectives listen to the accused person's side of the story. The accused doesn't have to talk unless a lawyer is present but may choose do so anyway.

The accused will be taken to a holding cell until he is arraigned. The investigation continues.

**Arraignment**

An arraignment is the legal process involved in bringing somebody before a court of law to answer a criminal charge. Bail is set at this time.

# Bail

The purpose of bail is to make sure the accused shows up in court. If the accused is in jail, detectives can be sure of a court appearance. But in the United States, an accused person is considered innocent until proven guilty. The accused has the right to be free on bail. Once bail is paid, the accused is released from jail.

Bail must be reasonable. A judge decides how much it will be. Several things must be considered before bail is set.

- How serious are the charges against the accused?

- What is the evidence?

- What kind of person is the accused?

- Does the accused have family and friends in the community?

- Has the accused shown up for court or skipped bail before?

- What is the accused person's financial situation?

A judge also decides whether there is anything else the accused must do before being released. For example, the accused may be required to stay away from a certain witness or may be required to go through counseling or mental health testing.

If the accused shows up in court, bail money is returned. If the accused doesn't show up, the money is lost.

In some cases, judges find reasons not to release the accused on bail. These include

- if the charge is first-degree murder.
- if the case requires a death penalty.
- if the judge believes the accused is a danger to the community.
- if the judge believes the accused will not show up for trial.

## The Police Lineup

The accused may be placed in a lineup. The accused person stands in a line with five or six other people in front of a one-way mirror. They can't see or hear the witnesses in the next room. But the witnesses can see the lineup.

Everyone in the line is about the same age, height, and weight; has similar hair color and style; and is wearing similar clothing. The accused does not stand out in any way.

Each person in the lineup holds a numbered square. Police ask witnesses to point out anyone they recognize in the lineup.

If there are several witnesses, they are not in the room at the same time. They are not allowed to talk to one another in between viewings. Police also change the order of the lineup between witnesses.

It is important that police officers follow strict rules when setting up a lineup. They want the witnesses to identify who they think they saw. But the officers must also protect the rights of the accused.

# In the Courtroom

Derek Reese wore an orange jumpsuit when he first appeared before Judge Klein.

"Derek Reese, you are accused of first-degree robbery and attempted murder," the judge said.

"I didn't do it," Reese interrupted.

"Do you understand these charges?" the judge asked.

"Yeah, man. But I didn't do it!" Reese said.

"Do you have a lawyer, Mr. Reese?" the judge asked.

"No. I can't afford one," replied Reese.

"The court will assign you a lawyer," Judge Klein said. "In the meantime, what is your plea?"

"I didn't do it!" Reese exclaimed. "Not guilty!"

## Civil Cases and Criminal Cases

When a case goes to trial, it may be a civil case or a criminal case. A civil case is a disagreement between individuals. It has to do with a person's rights. Personal injury, divorce, and child custody are examples of civil cases.

In civil cases, people who feel others have wronged them file charges. These people are the plaintiffs. Defendants are the people being charged.

Plaintiffs decide what they want from the defendants. Then the two sides go to court. The judgment is a decision in which damages are paid or that gives certain rights to one of the parties, such as the custody of a child. Only rarely does a defendant in a civil case go to jail.

In a criminal case, the defendant has been charged with a crime. An arraignment and a preliminary hearing are held before the case goes to trial. The plaintiff, or the accuser, in a criminal case is always the government. The local, state, or federal governments act on behalf of the people. So the convenience store case would be called the *People (or the State of _____) vs. Derek Reese.*

In a criminal case, the sentence is usually jail or prison time and/or a fine for breaking a law.

## Arraignment

After a suspect has been arrested, an arraignment hearing must be held within 48 hours. This is the first appearance before a judge for the accused. The judge reads the charges and the rights of the accused.

If the accused has hired an attorney, the attorney will speak. If the accused can't afford an attorney, this is when the court appoints one.

**Attorneys**

The prosecutor, or the prosecution, is the lawyer or lawyers representing the party taking legal action against the accused. In a criminal case, the prosecution represents the general population.

The defense is the lawyer or lawyers representing the accused, or defendant, in a court case.

The accused also enters a plea. There are four different pleas the accused can enter.

- **Guilty** The accused admits to doing the crime. The judge hands down a sentence, and that's the end of the case. There is no trial.
- **Not guilty** If a person pleads not guilty, that doesn't necessarily mean innocence. A person who pleads not guilty is saying the prosecutor needs to prove the charges. If the prosecutor cannot prove the charges in court "beyond a reasonable doubt," the person will be acquitted, or set free. Beyond a reasonable doubt means that the evidence must show that there is no one else who could have committed the crime or no other way that the crime could have happened.
- **Not guilty by reason of insanity** This plea means the accused may or may not be guilty of the charges because of a mental disorder. Because of this disorder, the accused didn't understand that a criminal act was done. When a person who pleads not guilty by reason of insanity goes to trial, there will be two separate issues to decide. Is the person guilty, and did that person have a mental disorder when the incident took place?
- **No contest** This means the person isn't pleading guilty or not guilty. But the accused will accept the court's decision on guilt.

If the accused person pleads anything other than guilty, the next step is a preliminary hearing or a grand jury hearing.

## Preliminary Hearing

A preliminary hearing generally takes place within 10 to 20 days after an arraignment. During a preliminary hearing, a judge reviews the charge or charges against the defendant. The prosecutor questions witnesses and shows the judge what evidence has been gathered against the defendant.

The defendant's attorney can cross-examine, or question, the prosecution's witnesses. The attorney can challenge the prosecution's evidence and present evidence to show that the defendant is not guilty.

The purpose of the preliminary hearing is for the judge to decide whether there's enough evidence for the case to go to trial. In most cases that come this far, a judge will decide there is enough evidence. Sometimes the defendant's attorney will even waive, or give up, the right to have a preliminary hearing.

## Grand Jury

In some states, a grand jury rather than a judge may decide whether there is enough evidence for the case to go to trial. A grand jury is a group of 12 to 18 citizens. They are randomly chosen from the community.

The prosecutor presents evidence to the grand jury. There is no judge. And the hearing is not open to the public.

The defendant can testify at a grand jury hearing. The defense attorney is not allowed in the grand jury room, so most defendants choose not to testify.

The grand jury hears the evidence and decides whether there is enough evidence to go to trial.

# Plea Bargaining

At some point, the prosecutor may offer the defendant a deal. This is called *plea bargaining*. The defendant may agree to plead guilty to lesser charges. For instance, a defendant charged with first-degree robbery and attempted murder might agree to plead guilty to just the robbery charge if the attempted murder charge is dropped. The sentence, or punishment, for just one crime would be less than a sentence for two crimes.

A plea bargain is a contract between the prosecutor and the defendant. If the defendant doesn't plead guilty as agreed, the prosecutor drops the offer. Then the defendant must go to trial on the original charge.

It can be helpful for the defendant to plea bargain before official charges are filed. If the police are still investigating the crime, the prosecution might accept a guilty plea to lesser charges than it would be willing to accept later. In other words, once all of the evidence is uncovered, the prosecution might not be willing to plea bargain.

# Jury Trial vs. Bench Trial

Everyone has the right to a jury trial. In a civil trial, a jury is made up of about 8 people. That number may vary from state to state. In a criminal trial, a jury is made up of 12 people.

People are randomly chosen from the community to make up juries. It is their job to hear the case and enter a verdict, or formal decision. In a civil case, the verdict is the damages, if any, to be awarded. In a criminal case, the jury hands down a verdict of guilty or not guilty.

In a civil trial, seven of the eight jury members must agree on the decision. In a criminal trial, all jury members must agree. If an agreement can't be reached, the jury is considered a "hung" jury. Then a new trial is ordered, and another jury hears the case.

A judge is in charge at a jury trial. The judge's duties include maintaining order in the courtroom and making final decisions on questions about the law that the attorneys might raise.

The judge does not decide whether the defendant is guilty or not guilty. That is the jury's job. The judge gives the jury a list of instructions that they must use when considering the verdict. These are legal guidelines that must be followed.

In a bench trial, there is no jury. A judge hears the case and decides whether the defendant is guilty or not. Bench trials are usually faster and cheaper than jury trials. But studies have shown that a jury is more likely to return a not-guilty verdict than a judge is.

## The Discovery Process

One stage of legal proceedings is the discovery process, which takes place before the trial. Each side has the right to know what information the other side has. The prosecutor must tell the defendant's attorney what evidence will be presented at the trial and what witnesses will be called. The defendant's attorney must do the same thing.

Once the defense sees the evidence the prosecutor has, the accused may want to plea bargain, if the prosecutor is willing, or continue to trial.

## A Criminal Trial

At the beginning of a trial, a judge reads the charges against the defendant and the plea that was entered. Then the prosecutor makes an opening statement. An opening statement tells the jury what the attorney is planning to prove during the

trial. The defendant's attorney may make an opening statement or wait until it's the defense's turn to present evidence.

The prosecutor calls witnesses and presents evidence first. The defendant's attorney can question the prosecutor's witnesses. This is called *cross-examination*.

When the prosecutor is finished presenting the state's case, the defendant's attorney calls witnesses and presents evidence on behalf of the defendant. The prosecutor can cross-examine those witnesses.

The defendant's attorney doesn't have to present any evidence at a trial. And the defendant does not have to speak. Remember, the accused is innocent until proven guilty. It is the prosecutor's job to prove the defendant's guilt beyond a reasonable doubt.

When both sides have presented all their evidence, they give closing arguments. Closing arguments summarize what went on during the trial. Both sides have one last time to present their side to the jury. Then the case is turned over to the jury. It's up to the members of the jury to decide whether the prosecution has proven guilt beyond a reasonable doubt.

● ● ●

"Ladies and gentlemen of the jury. Have you reached a verdict?" Judge Hill asked.

"We have, Your Honor," said the jury foreman.

The bailiff took a sheet of paper from the jury foreman. He handed it to the judge.

The judge opened the paper and read it to himself. Then he turned to Derek Reese, the defendant.

Reese rose to his feet.

# Index